W9-ACY-042

better together*

*This book is best read together, grownup and kid.

a kids book about™

adventure

by Ben Tertin

For Annabelle and Wesley,
my beloved.

Intro

As a parent, I instinctively want to give comfort and security to my kids. I want to protect them from failure and pain. And yet, I'm learning that this good, instinctive desire to keep them cozy can actually do them harm.

When I teach them to wonder, risk, attempt, learn, and grow, then I am teaching them how to open up and come alive.

However, when I teach them to chase comfort and security, I shut them off from reality. Worse, rather than helping them learn to live, I merely teach them to "get through" their days safely.

Deep down, we grownups want to help unpredictable little miracles explode into beautiful lives. We want to help develop and nurture an adventurous spirit within them.

That's why I wrote this book.

Once upon a time...

just kidding, this is not
that kind of story.

This is a story about...

My name is Ben.

I grew up with a small family in a little town that had a HUGE chocolate factory.

Really, it did...
and the whole town often smelled like cocoa.

My sister and I rode bikes and scooters and skateboards every day. We caught fish and frogs in the river. We played with our brown dog, Zeke, and built forts and swings in the woods.

Oh, and
we picked
lots of
raspberries,
too.

Sometimes
enough
to make a
pie!

Our town,
our home,
our street,
our woods,
our river,
and even the warm chocolate
smell in the air had all
become familiar.

Most days, we knew just
what to expect.

That felt good.

But then

To a new state.
To a new city.
To a new house.
To a new school.
To a new EVERYTHING.

Guess what I felt inside...

Do you ever feel afraid when you face something new?

Of course you do!
We ALL do.

Because we do not know what to expect.

We do not know what is going to happen.

But check this out:

NOT KNOWING WHAT WILL HAPPEN is the secret to *adventure.*

Here's the deal:

We ~~like~~ LOVE to know what is going to happen.

That's familiar, and that feels good.

But we get ~~worried~~ TERRIFIED when we don't know what will happen.

That worry is OK because it helps you pay attention to real danger.

adventure

does not mean careless or foolish.

adventure

means being smart and learning the difference between true danger and goodness.

When something is new, we quickly ask...

What if it doesn't work out?

What if they don't like me?

What if it tastes like onions?

What if I don't win?

What if they laugh at me?

What if this ends up
making me cry?

...because we're afraid of
what might happen.

Sometimes we worry about new schools, new towns, new teams, new foods, or even new families.

Sometimes we worry about big things, like flying in an airplane or learning to swim in deep water.

Sometimes small things, like reading new books or going to new places, can make us worry.

*This book might even be new!

So what should you do?
What should I do?!

Remember the secret to *adventure* is NOT KNOWING WHAT WILL HAPPEN.

When you don't know
what will happen,

and you feel that normal worry,

go ahead and think through
the bad things that
could happen,

but also WONDER about
the good things.

Instead of only asking:

"What if I fail?"
OR
"What if this ends poorly?"

You should also ask:

"Why not try?"
OR
"Why not see if this ends well?"

Like...

Why not try to make a
new friend?

Why not discover something
new about yourself or the
world around you?

Why not learn to play a new
sport, instrument, or
game with friends?

Saying...

"OK. Why not?"

Can help you come up with a million good things to hope for instead of a million bad things to worry about...

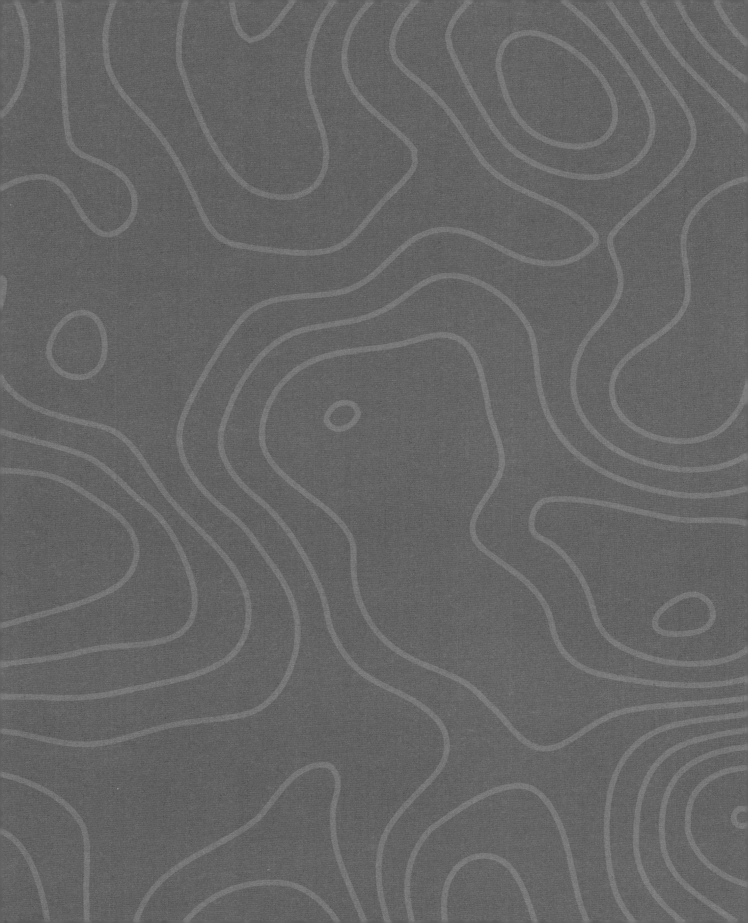

adventure

means being willing to try something new... growing healthy and strong as you do.

So try to remember these two words:

Why not?

New things come up all the time and you will worry (that's normal).

But try to never ONLY worry.

Remember to ask, "Why not?" And wonder about how this new thing might be awesome.

When you do that, you are headed for great *adventure*.

From a guy
who grew up
building tree forts
and rope swings in a
little town that smells
like chocolate, I say to you:
May your life be full of endless

Why not?

The End

Outro

Is adventure risky? Yes. Is it comfortable and secure? No and no.

Encourage your kiddo to take risks and do new things, because that's where true adventure happens.

Here are some ways you can do that:

1. Remind them of a time when they didn't want to try something new, but it ended up being amazing.

2. Tell them about a time when you were worried about some new thing and didn't try it because you asked "What if?" instead of "Why not?"

3. Challenge them to try one new thing TODAY! Something they would have said no to yesterday, but might be willing to try now.

Help them find a new adventure every day, and just maybe you'll find one, too!

find more kids books about

racism, feminism, creativity, money, depression, failure, gratitude, belonging, cancer, body image, and anxiety.

akidsbookabout.com

share
your read*

*Tell somebody, post a photo, or give this book away to share what you care about.

@akidsbookabout